2/15

Who's Got Next?

Future Leaders of America

By Ron Berman

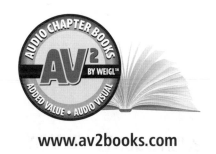

www.av2books.com

Your AV² Media Enhanced book gives you an online audio book, and a self-assessment activity. Log on to www.av2books.com and enter the unique book code from this page to access these special features.

Go to **www.av2books.com**, and enter this book's unique code.

BOOK CODE

Q235723

AV² by Weigl brings you media enhanced books that support active learning.

AV² Audio Chapter Book Navigation

HIGHLIGHTED TEXT   ACTIVITIES   HOME   CLOSE

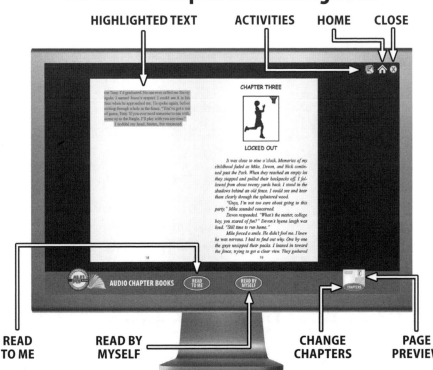

READ TO ME   READ BY MYSELF   CHANGE CHAPTERS   PAGE PREVIEW

Published by AV² by Weigl
350 5th Avenue, 59th Floor
New York, NY 10118

Website: www.av2books.com   www.weigl.com

Library of Congress Control Number: 2013937446
ISBN 978-1-62127-998-3 (hardcover)
ISBN 978-1-62127-954-9 (single-user eBook)
ISBN 978-1-48960-029-5 (multi-user eBook)

Printed in the United States of America in North Mankato, Minnesota
1 2 3 4 5 6 7 8 9 0   17 16 15 14 13

062013
WEP310513

TABLE OF CONTENTS

Joelle James of Murrieta, California, sings the national anthem.

A Kid with a Cause

Star Search

A sign hung on the dressing room door. It was the kind of sign that would usually have a famous name written on it—a name like Mariah Carey, Madonna, or Jennifer Lopez. Instead, in large bold letters, was the name Joelle James.

True, the dressing room was tiny, but that didn't matter. When Joelle opened the door and walked inside, she couldn't help but giggle. "Can you believe all of this?" she asked her mother. Mrs. James responded with a hug. They were both excited. After all, Joelle was about to sing on television for the first time. She was only twelve years old.

Carol Jones stepped inside the dressing room. She was one of the producers of the hit television show *Star Search*. Carol looked at the clipboard in her hand. She said to Joelle, "In a few minutes, somebody will be coming in to do your hair and make-up. You're going to be fantastic tonight!"

After Carol left, Mrs. James closed the door to the dressing room. Joelle started getting ready. It was then that she really began to feel the pressure. In less than two hours, she would be appearing on live television. For a moment, she became so nervous that she thought she might be sick. "Mom, I don't know if I'm going to be able to sing. I'm kind of freaked out right now."

"It'll be okay, honey," Mrs. James replied. Picking up a hairbrush from the table, she started combing Joelle's long blonde hair. "Once you get out on stage, you'll feel better. You're always nervous beforehand."

This was true. Joelle's nerves usually went away when she hit the stage. She had been singing in front of people since she was five years old. It had started simply enough, singing in the church choir. Back then it was only for fun, of course. Joelle just loved to sing—whether it was in the shower, at home with her family, or in front of other people.

Within a very short time, Joelle improved tremendously. Her parents quickly set her up with voice lessons. Joelle was determined to be the best singer she could possibly be. She knew that she wanted to make a career out of music. She daydreamed that one day she would sing in front of a large crowd. Joelle would sit in her room and listen to the radio for hours. She enjoyed singing along, pretending to be performing at a concert.

Right around Joelle's eleventh birthday, she got her first big break. She was invited to sing the national anthem at a baseball game. This was a good opportunity. Joelle hoped she could pull it off.

Getting up there in front of 10,000 fans was a new experience. "To be honest, it was pretty scary," Joelle recalls. "Once I hit that first high note, though, I really calmed down. I fell in love with performing in front of a big crowd."

A minute later, Joelle finished singing "The Star-Spangled Banner." The crowd cheered. Everyone in the stadium agreed that she had done a beautiful job. Joelle had every reason to feel proud. People were coming up to her to say how impressed they were with her singing.

Joelle was asked to sing the national anthem for many other sports teams. These included the Los Angeles Dodgers and the Los Angeles Lakers. She even appeared at a NASCAR racing event! Joelle had a blast every time. She was proud to sing America's national anthem. It was also fun going to sporting events with her family. It was especially cool going as a VIP (Very Important Person)!

Check out the sign on the door—when Joelle sang the national anthem at a NASCAR event, they picked her up in an official car!

Joelle, shown posing outside of her dressing room, prepares to sing on national TV.

A Promising Start

Today, Joelle was preparing to go on national television and sing on *Star Search*. This television show featured talented young performers. Before *American Idol*, *Star Search* was the most famous show for discovering new talent.

As Joelle sat in her dressing room, she wondered what would happen. For a moment, her mind raced wildly with scary thoughts: *What if my voice cracks? What if I trip and fall? What if I forget the words to the song? What if . . .*

"You're on in fifteen minutes, Joelle," Carol Jones said, poking her head in the door. She smiled and flashed a thumbs-up sign. Joelle, who had been lost in thought, quickly stood up. She turned around and looked at herself in the mirror.

At that instant, something clicked inside of Joelle. This was her moment, her big chance. It was not the time to be nervous. Joelle took a deep breath and looked at her mom. "I'm ready."

Joelle and her mother walked over to the backstage area. She would wait here with the other competitors. Everyone was watching the stage area, just a few feet away. Out in the audience, the crowd clapped and cheered for their favorite performers.

Getting the signal from Carol Jones, Joelle took her position just off the stage. It was from here that she would make her entrance. A taped interview that she had done before was showing on the large monitor. This would introduce Joelle to the audience. Then it would be up to her.

This was a moment that every performer can relate to—just seconds before walking out to face the crowd. Joelle was excited . . . and a little bit scared. She told herself to breathe normally and relax. As they announced her name, she smiled and walked out on the stage.

The huge crowd applauded. Joelle's family and friends were at home, sitting in front of their televisions. As Joelle started singing a song called "Think," she forgot about being nervous. She suddenly felt very comfortable. "When I'm singing and the crowd is into it, there's no place in the world I'd rather be."

Joelle was having a great time. This was one of

the largest stages she had ever performed on. There were bright lights and cameras all over the place. The floor of the stage was lit up. It was hard to see the audience because of the lights, but Joelle could hear them. They were extremely loud!

When Joelle sang the final note of the song, people jumped to their feet and cheered. Back home, her sister and brother were screaming with excitement. Their father started answering the telephone calls that were suddenly coming in. Mr. James's daughter was singing on television! She was a star!

A lot of people were impressed by Joelle's performance, including the judges. In fact, a celebrity guest judge was there that night—former NBA champion Magic Johnson. The "Magic Man" told Joelle, "Girl, you've got soul and attitude!" When Joelle heard this, she wondered if she was dreaming. But if this was a dream, it wasn't over yet. The judges added up their scores. Joelle had won—she was advancing to the next round! All of her hard work had paid off.

Joelle ended up making it all the way to the semifinals of the competition. A reporter asked if she was satisfied with her performance. "I know there's a lot of hard work ahead of me," Joelle said. "But tonight was a promising start to my career."

Balancing Act

Joelle James is now fifteen years old. She has definitely done some very cool things in her life. In her own mind, though, she's just a normal high school student. Her family lives in Murrieta, a small California town north of San Diego. Like most teenagers, Joelle likes to hang out with her friends. She also enjoys shopping at the mall and going to the movies.

Joelle knows that she has to make time for everything in her life. Her music career obviously requires a lot of work. Still, she doesn't let it take away from her schoolwork. "It's like a balancing act," she explains. "Music is my passion, but nothing is more important than my education. I have no way of knowing what's going to happen with my music career—but nothing is going to stop me from doing well in school."

That says a lot about Joelle. It would be easy for her to slack off in school and focus on her career. However, Joelle is too smart not to have a backup plan. Even though she's only a sophomore in high school, she's already thinking about college. She'll study music, but she's also interested in psychology and medicine. Those careers both involve working with people who need help. This is something Joelle cares about a great deal. She's already had the chance to help people through her work with ASB.

ASB stands for Associated Student Body. It's a club that organizes charity events, parties, and other things at her high school. Joelle has gotten involved in many ASB events. One of them was a Relay for Life 5K run. It brought students together to support cancer research. It was an awesome experience for Joelle, who always tries to make a difference. Maybe that's why she won a special award as the Kid of the Year.

Kid of the Year

Kids with a Cause is an organization in Los Angeles. Many young entertainers lend their time and support to it. Their goal is to help out less fortunate children. The most famous member of Kids with a Cause is actress and singer Hilary Duff.

Two awesome members of Kids with a Cause— superstar Hilary Duff and Joelle James.

Another awesome member of Kids with a Cause is Joelle James. She's always ready to help out. Joelle says, "Most kids don't realize how great their lives are. We have food to eat and warm beds to sleep in. But we never stop and think about how lucky we are.

It makes me sad to know how many kids don't even have *that*. It would be cool if every one of us did just a little bit of volunteer work. Think how much we could accomplish."

Joelle has done a lot of positive things for her community. For example, she sings at concerts to benefit Kids with a Cause. But it's not only about raising money for the organization. It's about trying to help people. That's what Joelle did when she met a little girl named Karen Gonzalez.

It all happened at a benefit concert for Kids with a Cause. Karen, a shy, brown-eyed ten-year-old, was seated in the second row. She was watching Joelle sing. Sadly, Karen's parents have both died and she lives in an orphanage. Although she is treated well and has friends there, life is hard for Karen. It's very tough when you don't have your own family.

When Joelle started singing that evening, Karen leaned forward in her seat. For some reason she felt very close to Joelle even though they had never met. Karen was drawn to Joelle's beautiful voice. She also loved the lyrics of the song Joelle was performing. When Joelle finished singing Mariah Carey's song "Hero," Karen's eyes were filled with tears. It almost felt like Joelle had been singing only to her. That's not unusual, because Joelle has that effect on many people. "It's awesome when I'm able to connect with somebody through a song," Joelle explains. "For me, music isn't about money or being famous—*that's* what it's all about."

After the concert that night, Karen nervously approached Joelle and asked for an autograph. Joelle smiled and handed her new fan a signed photograph. The real surprise, however, took place a few weeks later. Taking time out of her busy schedule, Joelle went to visit Karen at the orphanage. It was an amazing day for the little girl. She later said, "It made me feel very special." And the photo that Joelle signed for Karen? It's hanging on the little girl's wall, right by her bed!

Joelle James doing what she does best—inspiring people with her beautiful voice.

Joelle always downplays the cool things she does. She doesn't need attention for her charity work. However, it was only a matter of time before her work would be recognized. And it happened in a big way. In 2004, Kids with a Cause named her Kid of the Year! It was an honor that Joelle will always appreciate.

Joelle James may end up becoming a famous singer. Or, she may simply sing in the church choir. Regardless, she has begun an exciting journey. She makes a difference in the lives of people every single day—with her beautiful voice, and also with her beautiful spirit. It seems to call her to help out others. That's why she is a kid with a cause!

The Good Life

Having a Blast

Tyler Ribeiro was having a blast. He was riding along a dirt path on his motorcycle. It was a bright, sunny afternoon in Tulare, California. Tyler was just enjoying the moment.

Tyler is an easygoing teenager. He has a personality that is described by his friends as "chill." He also loves to have fun. There's nothing he enjoys more than hopping on his bike and taking off for a while.

Tyler continued riding along. He explored a back road and then zoomed through the fields. The wind whipped at his back. There was wide-open space as far as the eye could see. Tyler felt a wonderful sense of freedom and relaxation. The coolest part was that he didn't even have to leave his family's property. They own a farm that covers more than 700 acres!

The following morning, Tyler got dressed and strolled into the kitchen. He gulped down a tall glass of cold milk. Quietly, he walked out the back door and headed over to the barn. On a dairy farm that has more than 3,000 cows, something always needs to be done. Tyler does many things that help the farm run smoothly. On a busy day he might feed the calves and give medicine to a sick cow. He might also clean out a few stalls. Sometimes he will do all of this before he gets around to eating breakfast!

Sixteen-year-old Tyler Ribeiro of California, shown driving the tractor on his family farm.

Tyler looked around at the huge pen. Most of the cows were still sleeping. It was just past six o'clock in the morning. A crisp burst of cold air blew against Tyler's face. He zipped up the windbreaker he was wearing. Tulare can sometimes be cold and dark early in the morning.

The rest of Tyler's family was also awake. Even Tyler's younger brother and sister, Cameron and Gabrielle, had chores to do. On a farm, everyone pitches in as soon as they're old enough to walk. It's not all work, of course. Tyler had so much fun when he learned how to drive a tractor—at the age of seven! His father describes it this way: "The steering wheel was bigger than Tyler. It looked like an empty driver's seat with a baseball cap sticking out!"

Tyler and his family live and work at their family farm. It's called the Rib-Arrow Dairy. Besides all the animals, there are hundreds of acres of crops. They grow tons of alfalfa, corn, and winter wheat. The amazing thing is that *all* the crops are grown to feed the cows. The average cow eats 100 pounds of food and drinks up to forty gallons of water—every single day!

Feeding cows well and keeping them happy is a big part of dairy farming. That's what Tyler's family does. They care about the land, and about providing healthy food for people. That's why they own a dairy farm, which produces sweet, delicious milk.

Milking the Cows

A short while later, it was time to milk the cows. The first thing Tyler did was lead the cows into the Milking Parlor. This is where the cows are brought to be milked. This is done three times a day, usually eight hours apart. Cows do not mind being milked and it doesn't hurt them at all. However, the process takes time. It has to be done correctly to produce fresh, clean milk.

Tyler has been milking cows practically his entire life. He knows exactly what to do. He explains that milk is stored in the cow's udder. This is the organ that looks like a large bag. Milk flows from the four "teats," or nipples, that are connected to the udder. The teats are first washed and cleaned. Then they are attached to a milking machine. This machine sends the milk to a huge container that keeps it cold and fresh. The milk is then shipped to a company that sells it for the Rib-Arrow Dairy.

"A lot of work goes into producing fresh milk," Tyler explains. It's worth it, though. As Tyler points out, it's not just milk. After all, what would a slice of pizza be without the delicious cheese? Cheese, of course, is made from milk. So are many of the other foods we eat every day. Ever stop to think about a frosty chocolate milkshake? Well, ice cream is made from milk. If there were no milk, there would be no ice cream. How about that baked potato with butter and sour cream? You guessed it . . . both butter and sour cream are made from milk! Cream cheese, buttermilk, whipped cream, yogurt, cottage cheese—the list goes on and on.

Tyler is right in saying that people don't think about how many uses there are for milk. People have gotten used to buying food at the market. They forget where food actually comes from. In the old days, people only ate what they were able to grow. It's worth remembering that food and clean water come from the land. That's one reason why it's so important to show respect for our world.

Tyler knows that even simple things, like not littering, make a big difference. He explains that farmers rely on the land for their living—and that's why farmers care so much about it: "If we take good care of our planet, it will take care of our needs in return."

The Life of a Farmer

Tyler Ribeiro was born to be a farmer. This way of life is something he appreciates more every single day. He realizes that he is part of a new generation. That's pretty cool, because his family has been farming for many years.

Thirteen-year-old Cameron looks on as big brother Tyler does a little repair work on the farm.

It all started with Jose Coehlo Ribeiro, Tyler's great-grandfather. Mr. Ribeiro left his home country of Portugal in 1920. He came over to the United States by himself on a boat. He was only seventeen years old at the time! He made his way to Los Banos, a city in California. Mr. Ribeiro got a job milking cows. Soon afterward he moved on, settling in the city of Tulare. In 1924 he sent for his three brothers. After they arrived from Portugal, the Ribeiro Brothers started farming together in Tulare. Now, more than eighty years later, their family is still there!

Tyler is doing what his father does—and his grandfather and great-grandfather did—before him. "It's cool that I'm going to carry on the family business," Tyler says. He wants to work on the family farm and eventually run it.

Mr. and Mrs. Ribeiro are determined to let their children make their own decisions in life. It's not even certain that Tyler's brother and sister will end up becoming farmers. It's something they'll have to decide in the future, as they get older.

Not Tyler. He's a farmer, no doubt about it. He loves animals, he's comfortable around machines, and he's not afraid of hard work. "I like being out in the field or working at the dairy," Tyler declares. "It's a lot of work, but all of us around here are used to it. We don't watch the clock. We just work until the job is done right."

This is a great attitude, because working on a farm isn't like a normal job. An example of this is the winter planting season. Sometimes the Ribeiros have to rush to plant the wheat ahead of a big storm. The only way to get it done is to work all through the night.

That's the life of a farmer, and Tyler loves it. "Living on a farm is awesome," he says. "In my opinion, it's a real nice way to grow up." It sure is. When Tyler is with his animals, or driving the tractor, he's a happy guy. He doesn't mind dirt on his face and mud on his shoes. He'll take that over a fancy suit any day!

When Tyler isn't riding around the farm on his motorcycle, you can usually find him at the dirt track, flying through the air!

Hobbies and Interests

Growing up in a farming community has been great for Tyler. He has many hobbies and interests that have nothing to do with being a farmer. Of course, he loves riding his motorcycle. Besides that, Tyler is a musician. He plays piano in the youth band at church. Music is definitely a fun hobby for Tyler—not just playing, but listening to it as well.

Living on a farm, Tyler has always had awesome pets. He smiles when he talks about his favorite dog, Rusty, who was a three-legged dog! After Rusty was hit by a car, his leg had to be amputated. That didn't break his spirit, though. He ended up living until he was almost sixteen years old. Tyler recalls, "Rusty was a great dog. He was huge, almost seventy-five pounds, and he sure ran funny. But what would you expect from a three-legged dog!"

Although Tyler is a happy and easygoing guy, he is also very smart. He and his parents take education very seriously. Farming is a serious business, just like any other career. Many hours are spent in the field or in the barn. But just as many hours are in front of a computer, or on the telephone. If Tyler expects to be running a farm one day, he'll have to be good in business. That's why he's definitely going to college.

Naturally, Tyler will take classes related to farming. In addition, he'll be taking several business courses. As he says, "You need to know everything. I want to learn how to make good deals for the milk, equipment, and other things. When the day comes that I'm in charge, I want to be ready."

Future Farmer of America

"I've grown up learning how to take good care of living things," Tyler says. This is true. Tyler and his family treat *all* their animals well. "We care about them," he continues. "We're concerned when they're sick, and we feel sad when they die. Our cows and our animals are important to us."

Tyler moves a calf.

The Ribeiros do a lot for their cows. They try to keep the barn cool in the summer and warm in the winter. They try to keep the barn dry and comfortable at all times. This shows kindness to the animals. It's also a known fact that happy and relaxed cows produce more milk.

In addition to everything else he does, Tyler is a member of Future Farmers of America. This organization educates kids about farming and many other things. It also gives Tyler a chance to meet other kids that are planning to become farmers.

Tyler is also involved with an organization called Young Life. He recently traveled with them to Mexico during spring break. He wasn't there to party—he was there to do something important. "It just felt like the right thing to do," Tyler says.

The purpose of the trip was to help out deserving families by building houses for them. Tyler and the other teenagers worked hard. They also found time to do many other cool things. For example, they visited a school for underprivileged children. Tyler and his friends sang to the kids in Spanish and played games with them. They even joined the kids at a huge barbecue! The trip was a great success. "It was incredible," Tyler recalls. "I'm planning to go back next year."

If Tyler says he's going back, you can count on it. That's just the kind of person he is. Farm life has been good for this caring, sincere, sixteen-year-old young man. His future is very bright.

One day Tyler will head off to college. He'll meet different people and enjoy new experiences. But don't expect this farmer to move to the big city permanently. Instead, look for him to return to Tulare. After all, the Ribeiros have been living and working there for nearly a century. Standing in the fields, talking, laughing, working, and playing—that's the good life to Tyler Ribeiro!

Planting his Roots
in Plant City

Thanksgiving

Henry Johnson's mouth was watering. Looking at the huge table, he couldn't decide what to eat first. There were platters of glazed ham, cornbread, sweet potato pie, and collard greens. Henry wished every day could be Thanksgiving!

Sixteen-year-old Henry and his parents live in Plant City, Florida. They also have a large family that is scattered all over the country. Holidays like Thanksgiving and Christmas are opportunities to come together. "Our family events are a lot of fun," Henry says. "And we all love to eat, so food is a big part of it."

It's not just about the food. This family has played an important role in Plant City. They have contributed to education and civil rights. So when the Johnsons get together, they talk about many things. It all adds up to a good time for everyone. For convenience, everybody brings something to share. "It's like a big potluck dinner," Henry says. "It's *always* fantastic."

Nobody had to ask what Henry's mom had prepared. Mrs. Johnson is famous for her red velvet cake. Henry loves it, but he does more than just eat it—he has also learned how to bake it. He has even won cooking contests with it!

It's great that Henry Johnson is so handy in the kitchen. At six foot four inches tall, he looks more like a basketball player. Henry *does* spend a lot of his time playing hoops. Still, he's not shy about his interest in baking. With his huge appetite, Henry learned something early on: if he wanted to eat, he needed to learn how to cook!

Sixteen-year-old Henry Johnson of Plant City, Florida, cooks up a delicious meal.

Henry remembers the first time he cooked for a lot of people. He was in the Boy Scouts and only eleven years old. He and another scout were given the job of cooking for the troop. Luckily, Henry already had some experience in the kitchen. The two boys whipped up a delicious meal. They made grilled chicken, vegetables, and a cake. Henry felt proud when fifteen hungry Boy Scouts ate every last bite of food.

That was a positive experience for Henry. It made him think about becoming a chef. He added it to his long list of future career choices. Whatever he does, Henry is sure about one thing. He wants to carry on his family's tradition of being involved in the community.

FCCLA

Two years ago, Henry was a freshman at Joe E. Newsome High School. He was in the homeroom of an excellent teacher named Mrs. Oburn. Henry mentioned his interest in cooking. Mrs. Oburn told him about some classes offered at school. They were known as Family Consumer Sciences. These classes taught things that would help teenagers when they became adults. Some of the topics were cooking, sewing, and how to be a good parent.

Henry decided to take these classes. This was important, because then he got accepted in FCCLA. That's short for Family, Career, and Community Leaders of America. FCCLA is an organization that focuses on issues that are important to young people. Members discuss many different topics, such as teen pregnancy and peer pressure. Another thing they do is give back to the community. That's a big part of FCCLA.

Henry and his friends in FCCLA did a lot of important things this year. They organized a Relay for Life walk to raise money for cancer research. They also took time out to visit a boys and girls club.

Henry feels good about everything he has done with FCCLA. He is always looking for a way to make a difference. His whole family is like that. They've had a big impact on Plant City—and on America.

Positive Influence

"I want to have a positive influence on people. That way of thinking comes from my parents, and also from Mrs. Gary." Henry is referring to a wonderful woman named Mrs. Ida Gary. She lived across the street from Henry until she passed away a few years ago. Mrs. Gary—or Granny, as Henry called her—was a dear friend of Henry's grandmother. She stayed close to the family, even after Henry's grandmother passed away.

A special bond developed between Henry and Granny. He learned a great deal from her. Granny had a sharp tongue and wasn't afraid to speak her mind. For several years, she served as president of the NAACP. That stands for National Association for the

Advancement of Colored People. It's a famous civil rights organization. Mrs. Gary had tremendous pride in her African American heritage. She also felt strongly about her community in Plant City. Henry feels the same way. He's proud of the role his family has played in Plant City.

Henry explains that it all started with Janie Bing. She was a woman who had the courage to stand up against racial segregation. In the years following the Civil War, some laws were passed in the United States. These laws restricted the rights of African Americans. The result was segregation, which means separating people based on race. African American people were limited as far as where they could eat, live, and work. It was extremely unfair.

There were many African American heroes who fought back against racial segregation. In the process, they put themselves in danger. Still, they demanded that *all* people be treated equal. These community leaders played a big role in changing America.

One of these brave people was Janie Bing. She just happened to be Henry Johnson's great-grandmother. In the 1920s, she opened up the Bing Rooming House and Restaurant. This was a boarding house that provided rooms for African Americans. A boarding house was like a hotel, except that it was somebody's house. The owner would rent out rooms and cook meals for visitors. Mrs. Bing realized that white people had their own boarding houses and restaurants. She decided to make sure that black people in Plant City did as well.

Henry stands in front of a Plant City landmark—the Bing Rooming House.

Henry is proud of all the important things his great-grandmother did. He's also proud of everything his family has done since then. Education is the key. Henry's mother is a teacher, as was his grandmother and great-grandmother. His great-uncle was a member of the county school board. He was involved in education and civil rights for a long time. In honor of his contributions, a school was named after him. It's called the E. L. Bing Elementary School.

Henry comes from a long line of teachers. So it's no surprise that teaching is yet another career choice he is thinking about. As Henry puts it, "I may very well end up as a teacher. But I want educate people no matter what career I choose." This makes sense when you realize that Henry loves talking to people. He is also interested in famous African American leaders of the past. He's fascinated by the ability they had to give powerful speeches. He might want to follow in their footsteps. So, although he might end up as a teacher—or a chef—Henry could also end up as a public speaker.

Public Speaker

When Henry was in the third grade, one of his classes focused on African American studies. The subject grabbed his interest right away. "My parents have always taught me to embrace my history and my culture," he says.

Henry did very well in the class, and in other subjects, too. As a matter of fact, his success in school led to a huge honor for him. At the age of eight, he became a member of the Thurgood Marshall Society. Thurgood Marshall was one of the most important African American leaders in history. As a lawyer, he won a famous case that made school segregation illegal. He later became the nation's first black member of the Supreme Court.

Henry, in accepting the honor, had to speak in

front of a thousand people! Amazingly, he didn't even feel nervous. He delivered an awesome speech. He talked about qualities such as faith, trust, and honesty.

With his proud parents at his side, eight-year-old Henry Johnson is inducted into the Thurgood Marshall Society.

Since then, Henry has gone on to do a lot of public speaking. He feels that it's a powerful way to express his point of view. Henry has been influenced by some of the leaders he admires. He speaks about the impact they have had on his life.

"I respect great African American leaders like Malcolm X and Marcus Garvey," Henry says. "They were men that spoke with incredible power and energy. They never worried about offending people. They talked about the need for equality for African

Americans." Henry has the potential to be a powerful voice for his community, too. He has even thought about going into politics. This career choice would make the most of his ability to communicate. It would also satisfy his desire to help people.

Henry has plenty of choices. He might be a politician—if he's not a chef or a teacher. Then again, he's an excellent athlete who plays many sports. That's yet another career possibility. . .

The Future

Sports have always been a big part of Henry's life. It started pretty simply. "When I was a kid, I was into the Power Rangers," he remembers. "Because of that, I decided to take karate." Eventually, he decided to give it up to play other sports.

By age ten, Henry was playing flag football. He then added basketball and soccer. However, in the eighth grade he had to drop football and soccer. It happened because of an interesting twist of fate. Henry, then thirteen years old, had grown to be a full six feet tall. His size and strength scared kids in his grade. Parents worried that Henry would accidentally hurt their children out on the field!

In the end, there was a happy outcome to this problem. Henry started devoting most of his time to basketball. He still liked football and soccer, but basketball was his favorite. He is currently a junior at Newsome High. For the last two years, he has played on the junior varsity squad. There's no doubt that Henry will earn a spot on varsity before long. He knows he's going to have to put in a lot of work to be ready. "The players in our county are huge. I'm going to be one of the guys banging with them down low."

Henry in his Newsome High uniform.

To prepare for next season, Henry plans to spend a lot of time in the weight room. He may also return to soccer. It's fun, and it helps him improve his footwork. He hasn't left football behind, either. Right now, his focus is on basketball, of course. But he has thought about possibly switching to football. He will decide by the time he reaches college. Henry loves all sports, so he can't lose no matter what he does. It makes sense to play the one he shows the most promise in.

Henry would be thrilled to be a pro basketball or football player. It's not because of the money or fame, though. He wants to make a difference in the world. Henry knows that people listen to star athletes. So hopefully he'll be lucky enough to be a pro. If so, he will use his fame to spread a positive message.

It's hard to know what career Henry will end up in. There's no way to predict where life will lead him. But wherever he goes, he'll be out there doing good work—not only for the African American community, but also for the entire country.

Henry Johnson sets a good example for the rest of us. He comes from an amazing family. They've been involved in education and civil rights for a long time. Look for Henry to carry on their fine work. Henry is planting his roots in Plant City. His family is already very proud of him. In the future, he will make his country proud as well!

Proud American: sixteen-year-old Chris Forsell of South Burlington, Vermont.

Fire and Rescue

Fire Alarm

Sixteen-year-old Chris Forsell was standing in front of South Burlington High School. He was talking and laughing with his friends. School had just let out. Everybody was hanging around, making plans for the weekend. Chris looked over at his buddy, Trevor. He said, "Dude, I'm learning this new song on guitar. Have you ever heard of . . ."

In the middle of this sentence, Chris's pager began to beep. It caught him by surprise. This was the first time the special pager had ever gone off. It was from the firehouse! Chris practically jumped out of his shoes. "I have to get over to the fire station right away," he said.

The guys all looked at Chris with respect. "Be careful, man," Trevor said, slapping five with his friend. Chris tried to contain his excitement. He quickly gathered his backpack and cell phone. In a flash, he was off.

By the time Chris got to the fire station, the trucks were already being loaded. He geared up. That means changing into a firefighter's uniform. Chris took a deep breath, trying to get his nerves under control. His heart was racing and his palms were sweaty. First, he put on his bunker pants and boots. Then he grabbed his heavy fire coat and yellow helmet. He was ready to roll.

This was not a training exercise. This was *real*. Earlier in the day, a fire alarm had gone off over at the mall. It had been reported as a false alarm, so no fire trucks were sent out. However, the alarm then went off a second time. This time, the firefighters didn't want to take any chances. They decided to rush down there just in case something was going on. A lot of people, including small children, were at the mall— and firefighters know how quickly a tragic situation can develop.

Chris Forsell is a member of the SBFD Junior Firefighter Training Program. SBFD stands for South Burlington Fire Department. This program gives qualified teenagers the opportunity to learn what firefighters do. First, Chris and the other teenagers had to go through an intense period of training. Then they were given their official gear.

The fire truck sped through the city streets with its siren blaring. Chris, sitting in the fire truck, could still feel his heart pounding. He was finally getting his first taste of this thrilling career. Chris has always been in awe of the bravery that firefighters show. These courageous men and women face danger every day. They save lives, help people, and battle one of nature's deadliest forces—fire. They perform a great public service. Firefighters are the people running *into* a burning building when everybody else is running out.

Chris admires these heroes, and he wants to join them someday. That's why he was so happy about being accepted into the SBFD training program. There's no doubt that his life as a firefighter will be filled with excitement and danger. But that's not all. He'll have the chance to be a hero … just like the members of the South Burlington Fire Department.

Firefighting

Luckily, Chris's first go-around as a junior firefighter ended up being easy. When they arrived at the mall, the firefighters looked all around. They made sure that there was no fire anywhere. Meanwhile, Chris stayed on the ground outside the mall. He directed traffic and kept an eye on the truck. He was also in charge of the radio. If one of the firefighters needed a piece of equipment, they would ask him for it.

It didn't take long to figure out what had caused the alarm to go off. It was simply a failure of the alarm system. Chris's first call wasn't an actual fire. Still, it was a great beginning to his career. When it was over, he was pumped. Chris was on his way to being a real firefighter. This is something he's been dreaming of for a long time. A *very* long time.

Chris's interest in this career began when he was quite young. He can still remember watching a video about firefighting called "Fire and Rescue." It showed smoke coming out of a building that was on fire. As the firefighters raced through the hallways, Chris was on his feet cheering. "I loved that video," Chris remembers. True, it was nothing more than entertainment for him at that point. But it did raise his interest in firefighting.

Another big influence is his father. Mr. Forsell is the safety officer with the South Burlington Fire Department. That position has placed him at the scene of many fires. His job is extremely important. "Firefighters are concerned about helping other people," Chris explains. "They sometimes don't even think about themselves. That's where my dad comes in. He's there to protect *them*. He'll make sure that conditions are safe for them."

Often times, when Mr. Forsell is at home, he will get paged. That means he has to rush to a fire.

Chris always wants to ride along. A common question in the Forsell household is, "Dad, can I come with you?" Mr. Forsell has been hearing this question for many years. The cool thing is that it's not only Chris who is always asking! His older sister Becca is also interested in fire service. She is in the SBFD Junior Firefighter Training Program with Chris.

Chris and older sister Becca are both youth firefighters.

Chris recalls one of the times he was allowed to ride along with his father. It happened when he was thirteen years old. Chris and his dad were at a Boy Scout meeting. Suddenly, Mr. Forsell's pager went off. In a flash, he and Chris left the meeting and ran toward the parking lot. As all of the scouts watched in awe, they jumped into their car and drove off. With the red lights flashing on top of his car, Mr. Forsell drove quickly.

"What's the situation, Dad?" Chris asked.

"Big fire over at the auto body shop," Mr. Forsell replied. As they drove, he reminded Chris about safety procedures.

As soon as they arrived, Mr. Forsell dressed in his fire gear. He then went over to talk to the SBFD captain. Meanwhile, the firefighters were moving through the burning building. They wanted to see if any people or animals were trapped inside. Chris watched from the car. As always, he was fascinated. There was smoke and fire everywhere. It was scary, but the firefighters were calm as they battled the blaze.

The firefighters ended up doing a fantastic job. They contained the fire and prevented it from spreading to other buildings. Happily, nobody was injured or killed. "Firefighters are remarkable," Chris says. "They face life and death situations every day. The concentration and physical strength it takes to do their job is amazing. That's what motivates me. One day I'm going to be out there on the front line with them."

Summer Camp—with a Twist

For the last two years, Chris Forsell has gone to a fun summer camp. But there's a twist. It's a camp for future firefighters. For Chris, it's the best of all worlds. He gets to go to an awesome camp. He also gets to learn more about his career choice.

Forty-four kids usually come to camp, which lasts one week. It's located in Pittsford, Vermont. That's about fifty miles from Chris's home in South Burlington, Vermont. The campers range in age from fourteen to eighteen. They learn firefighting and emergency service skills. They also learn about teamwork. As Chris knows from experience, these are critical to being a good firefighter.

The camp combines fun activities with important firefighting lessons. An activity from last summer sticks out in Chris's mind. "It was a huge scavenger hunt," he says. Of course, being a fire camp, there was a twist: while trying to find the hidden items, the campers had to wear an SCBA. That stands for self-contained breathing apparatus.

Learning how to move around with the SCBA.

When firefighters run into a building, they obviously need fresh air to breathe. That's why they wear an SCBA. It's a unit that is attached to their face and back. It provides them with fresh air. Learning how to move around with it is tricky. This was an excellent opportunity for the campers to get used to it. It was a terrific learning experience. Chris reports that the scavenger hunt was also a lot of fun.

Chris goes to the camp because he learns important information. As a bonus, he's made new friends. "I've met so many cool people from all over Vermont," he says. "It's like being part of a whole new family for a week each year. We have an awesome time. We swim, fish in the pond, play ultimate Frisbee, and just hang out. This is a perfect camp for any kid who is interested in becoming a firefighter."

Chris and his friends conduct an outdoor practice drill at fire camp.

The Most Important R.A.C.E. of Your Life

"Fire is very dangerous. But if you learn a few things, one day you just might save somebody's life. Maybe even your own." Chris is right. That's why he offers a quick reminder about R.A.C.E.. It stands for rescue, alarm, contain, evacuate. He explains it in an easy way.

R is for rescue, which is what to do upon discovering that there's a fire. "Scream loudly to attract attention," Chris says. "If a door is closed, feel it before opening it. If the door is hot, DO NOT OPEN IT!" Instead, look for a window or some other way to get out. Next is A, which stands for alarm. "Make sure everybody else knows about the fire," Chris urges. "If your parents are asleep, run and wake them. Call 911 as soon as possible from a safe location."

Chris continues with C, which stands for contain. This means trying to prevent the fire from spreading. Chris advises quickly closing any doors that lead to the area of the fire. Finally, E is for evacuate, which is simple: get out of the house or building. Get away from the fire, and help the rest of your family make it to safety. Don't hide under your bed or in the closet. Never go back into the building!

Chris realizes that most people don't think about these things too much. The secret, he claims, is to learn about it first—before there is an actual fire. He also recommends that families have practice fire drills. That's the best way to prepare in case a real fire alarm ever goes off. "Everybody in the family should know where to go and what to do," Chris says. "That's what planning in advance, and R.A.C.E., is all about."

On His Way

Between fire camp and the Junior Firefighter Training Program, Chris Forsell is a busy guy. That's not all, though. He has plenty of other things going on also. He's already starting to think about college. Among other things, he plans to take a fire science class in college. It will help him prepare for his career.

After discovering a talent for drawing, Chris has developed a strong interest in art. He likes hanging out in the imaging lab at school. He works with advanced computer programs to create 3D images of characters. They can be used in video games, animation, and movies. This high-tech art is the wave of the future, and Chris is having a blast with it.

In addition to art, music is also a passion. Two years ago Chris started learning guitar. He's made steady progress ever since. As a matter of fact, he is already playing in a band. They are known as Three Pages Short.

Chris Forsell will be doing a lot of cool things in the years to come. He'll be playing his guitar and creating awesome art. Without a doubt, he'll also be continuing on his way to an exciting career. Sure, sometimes he thinks about the danger of being a firefighter. How many people have jobs that could cause them to get burned, or even killed? Chris insists that these fears won't stop him. "Being a firefighter is an adventure," he says. "You know the risks, you understand what could happen."

Chris is right. That's one of the things that make firefighters heroes. They are brave individuals. They do everything possible to save lives and reduce damage. Chris sums it up by saying, "I think I can make a real difference. It feels good to know that people will be counting on me."

That might be the quality that makes Chris Forsell so special. He has a real desire to help his community. Yes, people will be counting on him in the future . . . and he'll respond. Where there's fire, or somebody needs to be rescued, Chris will be there. He's looking forward to joining the brave firefighters that proudly serve South Burlington—and America.

Chris, in full gear, participates in a demonstration.

Dancing Through It All

The Competition

Lindsay Harwell stepped out of the hotel lobby with her teammates. It was hot and sunny. That's typical Florida weather, even for late January. Sipping from bottles of water, the girls waited for the bus. They were on their way to an outdoor stadium. That's where the most important dance competition of their lives was being held.

Lindsay Harwell of Southaven, Mississippi, showing flawless technique as she performs at the Universal Dance Association National Competition.

There was a lot of pressure. The best dance teams from across America were in Florida. They were all competing in the Universal Dance Association National Competition. Lindsay and her teammates were from DeSoto Central High School. They were representing their school and their hometown of Southaven, Mississippi. They wanted to make their friends and families proud.

DeSoto Central was definitely considered an underdog. Nobody expected the team to finish in the top ten. But they had a lot of motivation. They wanted to do their best in support of their teammate, Lindsay Harwell. Considering everything she was going through, she deserved it. This was a dark and difficult time in her life.

An hour later, the first round of the hip-hop competition began. The girls from DeSoto Central lined up on stage and waited. Then, as the first beat from their mix-tape dropped, they sprang into action. Team captain Kendall Lancaster led them through the fast-paced moves. Each one matched the beat of the music.

When the music ended, the dancers from DeSoto Central smiled brightly. The crowd rewarded them with a standing ovation! Waving as they left the stage, Lindsay and her teammates ran over to the side. They felt that they had done a good job, but now the other teams would get a turn. The judges would then decide which teams would advance to *the finals.*

A couple of hours later, the first round was complete. All of the teams had performed well. The girls from DeSoto Central nervously awaited the decision of the judges. They wanted the chance to dance again—not just for their school, but also for Lindsay.

Total Shock

Seventeen-year-old Lindsay Harwell has been dancing for as long as she can remember. As a matter of fact, she started dance and gymnastic lessons at the age of two! In the years that followed, her interest in dancing grew.

The future seemed bright for Lindsay. Suddenly, however, the life she had been living was turned upside down. It was less than two months before the national dance competition in Florida. "It was a total shock," Lindsay says. "Everything changed after I got the news."

It all started while preparing for the competition. Dancers go through intense physical training to get quicker and stronger. Pain, soreness, and injuries are a part of their lives. So when Lindsay noticed pain in her hip after practice, she didn't worry about it. She figured it would go away, just like any other minor injury. Unfortunately, it didn't.

After a while, Lindsay realized that this deep, sharp pain was getting worse. It was different than anything she had felt before. Her hip was so stiff that she was having trouble moving around. When Lindsay finally told her mother about it, Mrs. Harwell was concerned. She immediately took Lindsay to the doctor, who ran a test. And then another. He then recommended that Lindsay undergo a test called a bone scan. The entire process was exhausting, painful, and scary.

Finally, Lindsay found out what was causing her pain. The doctor explained that there was a large tumor near her hip. Lindsay had cancer.

Looking back, it's remarkable how far Lindsay has come. She has bravely fought against this deadly disease. It wasn't easy, especially on that first terrible day. When Lindsay got home, she was upset and scared. For that reason, she asked to sleep in her mother's bed. But sleep was hard to come by. Late at night, Lindsay was crying and wondering what was going to happen to her.

"I was caught up in so many different emotions," she recalls. "Finally, I decided that I had to just face this thing head on. I realized that I had no choice but to overcome my fears and deal with it." That's exactly what she did.

Lindsay immediately moved forward with chemotherapy. This is a treatment in which powerful drugs are pumped into a person's body. These drugs kill harmful cancer cells before they can spread to different parts of the body. The human body is made up of millions of cells. Cancer cells do not grow in a normal way . . . and once these destructive cells spread, they kill everything in their path.

Chemotherapy is a difficult treatment to go through. That's because the powerful drugs destroy *all* cells—not just the cancerous ones. As a result, patients undergoing this treatment often feel sick and weak. They usually lose their hair as well. The side effects are harsh sometimes, but chemotherapy can be very effective. It has saved many lives.

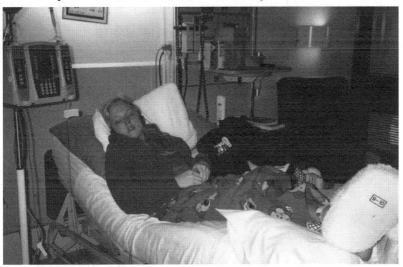

Lindsay listens to music during a chemotherapy treatment.

Lindsay would have to go in for treatments regularly. She was relieved to hear that she could still dance—if she felt strong enough. She also had another concern. "I knew I was going to lose my hair. I was worried that people would feel weird around me." As it turned out, Lindsay had nothing to worry about. She has always had amazing friends. Nobody acted strangely around her or treated her differently. The girls from the dance team even collected money to buy her a pretty blonde wig! Things were starting to look up. Still, Lindsay wasn't sure how she would feel. She didn't know if she could help DeSoto Central in the dance competition.

Turning Point

The girls were nervous. They were still waiting to find out if they had advanced to the finals. Lindsay was nervous, too. Win or lose, however, it was awesome just to be up on stage. She had undergone a chemotherapy treatment only a few days earlier!

Suddenly, the announcer asked all the competitors to come down to the main floor. Lindsay and the rest of the girls stood together and held hands. Emotions were running high. They wanted to hear "DeSoto Central" over the loudspeaker. They got their wish: they were one of the first teams announced for the finals!

The girls went crazy, hugging, laughing, and crying all at the same time. DeSoto Central was among the very best high school dance teams in the country. They were ready to celebrate! Lindsay and her teammates had fun that night, but got to bed early. They wanted to be sharp the next day for the final round of the competition.

The next morning, the DeSoto Central High School dance team arrived at the stadium. They were feeling great. It was a beautiful day and the crowd was pumped up. The girls were ready to dance. When their turn came, they pulled off an exciting routine. It had the fans on their feet.

For Lindsay, this performance was yet another high point. She hadn't been sure that she wanted to go to Florida. This was understandable. She hadn't known how she would feel.

Participating in the competition turned out to be a great decision. It became a turning point in Lindsay's fight against cancer. She knew that it wouldn't stop her from doing the things she loved. It certainly wasn't going to stop her from being the popular, friendly teenager that she is.

During the awards ceremony, Lindsay received another honor. As the announcer gave the results, the captains came up to the stage. They received a trophy on behalf of their teams. It was announced that DeSoto Central High School had finished fourth. The girls all screamed with excitement. They had worked very hard. Now they were one of the top four teams in the country.

Team captain Kendall Lancaster started to walk up to the stage. Suddenly, she stopped and looked over at Lindsay. "Come up with me to get the trophy," Kendall said. "You deserve it, Lindsay." The girls all started clapping. Some of them were *crying tears of joy. It was satisfying that they had placed so high in the competition. That was nothing compared to the joy of knowing that Lindsay was with them. To the cheers of the crowd, Lindsay held up the trophy.*

Smiles all around as the members of the DeSoto Central High School dance team pose with their hard earned, richly deserved trophy.

The Sound of Music

When Lindsay returned from Florida, she was on top of the world. The trip had been fun and exciting. It had also proven to her that she could still achieve her dreams.

Before being diagnosed with cancer, Lindsay had gone on an audition. It was for a spot in a musical called *The Sound of Music*. She had won a role as one of the nuns. She had been looking forward to the play for a long time. After her diagnosis, she wasn't sure if she would have the strength. But after her performance in Florida, she knew she could do it. "I'm not a quitter," Lindsay says. "This was something I had dreamed about doing. I wasn't going to let anything stop me."

Calm and cool up on stage, Lindsay, on the far right, performs in *The Sound of Music.*

On the opening night of the musical, Lindsay was nervous. However, when she finally got out on stage, everything seemed to fall into place. Lindsay gave a terrific performance. It was her first taste of what it takes to perform in professional musical theater. She plans to pursue singing and acting in the future along with her dancing.

While all of this was going on, Lindsay's family was up to something *big*. It started with some excited whispering. Lindsay also thought she saw her mother make a few secret phone calls. Everyone tried to pretend that nothing was happening, but Lindsay was suspicious. Her mom woke her up early on a Sunday morning to attend services at Colonial Hills. That wasn't even their normal church. Lindsay knew something was up. She just couldn't figure out what!

Lindsay arrived at church with her mom and dad, her brother Jordan, and her sister Lauren. She noticed right away that many other members of her family were also present. Looking around, Lindsay saw that the girls from the dance team were there as well. They were all smiling—*way* too much.

Toward the end of the service, the mayor of Southaven stood up. His name was Greg Davis. Lindsay had met the mayor before. She had been a student in a class taught by Suzanne Davis, his wife. Mrs. Davis was a wonderful woman. She had been very supportive of Lindsay, especially through the tough times.

After greeting everybody, the mayor started talking about Lindsay. He then turned to a large video monitor. He asked everyone to shift his or her attention to the screen. All of a sudden, a man named David Cutcliffe appeared on the screen. He was the head coach of the Ole Miss football team. Lindsay gasped. This was a big deal because she has always been a huge fan of the Ole Miss Rebels. They are an awesome college football team in the state of Mississippi. Lindsay couldn't believe this was happening.

Coach Cutcliffe talked about the Make-A-Wish Foundation. It is an organization that grants wishes to kids that are suffering from illnesses. He explained that it had done a lot for kids from Mississippi. Then he dropped the big news: Lindsay and her family had been granted a wish—they were going to Hawaii! The coach ended his speech with a smile, saying, "Aloha!"

This was a truly emotional moment. Lindsay was excited, happy and grateful. She started crying, as did the mayor and his wife, and everyone else. These were tears of happiness, of course.

Lindsay had shown great courage during her battle with cancer. People had been, and still were, inspired by her determination. Members of her community had an idea. They encouraged Lindsay's mom to send in an application to the Make-A-Wish Foundation. Mrs. Harwell knew that Lindsay had always dreamed of going to Hawaii. She decided to give it a shot. Mayor Davis and his wife sponsored the wish—and it had come true!

It seems as if many of Lindsay's wishes are coming true. After experiencing the lowest of lows, her life has been on the rise ever since. She is winning her fight against cancer every single day. "Life will test you," Lindsay explains. "You have to stand up and meet the test." She hopes that all kids will keep that in mind when they are faced with difficult situations.

Lindsay Harwell is a beautiful and talented dancer. She moves through life with the sound of music all around her. Of course, there have been times when the music has been mellow and sad. Still, she has performed with grace. Maybe that's why she inspires so many people. As her journey continues, expect the music of her life to be loud, upbeat, and fun. And expect to find Lindsay smoothly dancing through it all with a big smile on her face.

Aloha! Lindsay makes a new friend in the spectacular waters of Hawaii.

The Reporter

Sixteen-year-old Bryan Roy of Agawam, Massachusetts.

Searching the Moment

Bryan Roy watched as the cover was removed from the huge trophy. His heart was racing. It felt like things were happening in slow motion. Finally, Bryan got his first glimpse of it. He couldn't believe his eyes. He was staring at the most beautiful thing he had ever seen. His jaw dropped and he froze, unable to move.

The trophy was made of sterling silver. It was stunning. There were flags on it, representing every team in major league baseball. The trophy was heavy, too. Bryan was told that it weighed close to thirty pounds. Naturally, it was an expensive item. To Bryan, it was priceless. This trophy was the reason that people had gathered here at the Agawam Public Library.

Bryan had arrived at the library early. He wanted to make sure that he got a good spot in line. Hundreds of people from all over the town of Agawam began showing up. Bryan was amazed by what he was seeing. The library was normally quiet, but today it was alive with excitement. Everyone wanted to set their eyes on an awesome prize . . . the World Series trophy. Boston Red Sox fans had waited almost *100 years* for this. In 2004, the Red Sox had finally won their first championship since 1918!

"It's much more than just a trophy," Bryan explains. "Being a Sox fan isn't just about watching baseball. It's about family, tradition, and history." This is definitely true for the Roy family. The love of baseball has been passed down from generation to generation. Like Bryan, both his father and grandfather have always been devoted Red Sox fans. They were all together, watching the final game of the World Series.

When the Red Sox won, there was a lot of happiness in the Roy household. It was no different all across the state of Massachusetts. The celebration lasted a lot longer than just one night. Fans were thrilled to find out that they could actually see the trophy. It would be taken to each of the 351 cities and towns throughout the state. The latest stop was the Agawam

Public Library.

Many years earlier, Bryan's dad had taken him to his first Red Sox game. They had gone to historic Fenway Park in Boston. Eight-year-old Bryan was hooked. That night he became a Sox fan for life. "My first walk up Fenway Park's concourse ramp is something that I'll never forget. To this day, the rush still hasn't worn off."

Standing in the library, Bryan was feeling that very same rush again. He wasn't the only one. The happy crowd stared at the trophy, and cheered, "Let's go Sox." Seeing all the excitement around him, Bryan's mind started to wander. That's not unusual, because Bryan is more than a baseball fan. He is also a talented journalist.

A journalist is a person who collects, writes, and reports the news. For Bryan, as well as other reporters, every event is a possible story. Especially an event that places the World Series trophy just a few feet away! Bryan was searching the moment for a story.

Bryan is a reporter, and a huge Red Sox fan. He also loves to play the game of baseball. He's a member of the Agawam High Brownies. Bryan is looking forward to another good season. He's a solid hitter and a dependable outfielder. Still, no matter where he is, Bryan Roy is always searching the moment. He's looking for the story that needs to be told.

Bryan's greatest skill is the unique way he sees the world. He's good with a bat on his shoulder, but even better with a pen in his hand.

The Spruce News

When Bryan was ten years old, he came up with a great idea. By then he had already been a sports fan for many years. While most kids were watching cartoons, he was watching SportsCenter on ESPN. He was always up to date on scores, as well as news about his favorite teams.

Bryan's love of sports was handed down to him by his father. With each passing year, however, another interest was taking shape. It started almost as soon as Bryan was old enough to read and write. He discovered that he enjoyed expressing himself with words. Soon he began writing about anything that captured his imagination.

Bryan quickly decided that he wanted a career in journalism. He wanted to work as a reporter for a newspaper. By the time his tenth birthday rolled around, he decided to pursue his idea. Bryan Roy was going into the newspaper business. He was going to publish some of the stories he had been writing. He would call the newspaper *The Spruce News*.

Did his friends laugh at his idea? "Absolutely," he says with a smile. "But I think kids shouldn't be afraid to try new things. You have to just go for it sometimes. I'm really glad I did."

Bryan quickly learned that running a newspaper is hard work. The first step, naturally, was to come up with stories. As a growing writer, Bryan had that part covered. "At first I just wrote about things like sports and school. Eventually, I started including local news stories and current events."

Bryan would write the stories and then print them out on his computer. The next step was folding them so they looked like a real newspaper. Then he would mail them out. Among his subscribers were family members. They all looked forward to getting their copies of *The Spruce News*.

This was Bryan's first taste of the newspaper business. It helped him develop his interest in becoming a journalist. At ten years old, he was on his way.

The Spruce News, the newspaper Bryan created when he was only ten years old.

High School Reporter

After producing *The Spruce News*, Bryan was ready to take things to the next level. When he was in the seventh grade, he worked on his junior high yearbook. He wasn't allowed to write stories, though. Instead, he was made junior editor. "I worked with the main editors to prepare the yearbook for publication," he explains. "But I kept on writing because I knew that one day I would get my shot."

Bryan was right. The turning point came two years later, during his freshman year of high school. He signed up for a journalism course. "It had a big impact on me," Bryan recalls. "For the first time, I learned the *real* process of putting a newspaper together. It was very cool."

After completing the course, Bryan immediately enrolled in Journalism 2. It didn't take long before his articles began finding their way into the *Agawam Mirror,* the school paper. This was a great accomplishment for Bryan, who was still only a freshman. Determination and hard work had put him in a position to do what he loved. He had every reason to feel proud.

The Republican

What in the world am I doing here? Bryan stood nervously in front of a closed door. He was trying to work up the courage to open it and walk through. Adjusting his tie, he glanced up at the sign that said The Republican. That was all the motivation he needed. Taking a deep breath, he walked inside.

Bryan was still only a fifteen-year-old freshman. He was now a reporter for his school newspaper. He had no reason to aim higher. But Bryan is an ambitious teenager. He decided to try to get a job . . . writing for a big-city newspaper.

That's right, a teenager writing for a real newspaper. Not a school paper and definitely not *The Spruce News*. It was a total long shot, but Bryan sent out letters to every newspaper in the area. "I figured I didn't have a chance of hearing back from anyone," he laughs. Two weeks later, though, he received a phone call at his house. It was from a well-known newspaper called *The Republican*. He was invited to come in for a job interview.

When Bryan entered the busy newsroom, adults stared at him with curiosity. A few minutes later, he found himself sitting in Cynthia Simison's office. She would be interviewing him for a possible job at *The Republican*. Cynthia was a skilled newswoman herself. She was in charge of a section of the newspaper that reported on local news.

The interview went well. Cynthia asked Bryan about his background and experience. She then explained to him that working for a newspaper involves a *lot* of pressure. She couldn't hire him unless she felt he could perform at a high level. As the interview ended, they shook hands. Cynthia told Bryan that he would be hearing from her soon.

The days following the interview seemed endless. Bryan waited to find out if he had made the cut. Then, suddenly, Cynthia Simison called with fantastic news. *The Republican* was offering Bryan a job! Because he had school, he could work from home during the school year. In the summer, Bryan would actually work in the newsroom.

Just like that, Bryan was a reporter for an important newspaper. He couldn't have been more thrilled. "It's cool doing it at school, of course. I know I'm writing for all my friends and fellow students," Bryan says. "But at *The Republican* I'm writing for an entire town. That's a huge responsibility—and I'm up for it."

Hard at work, ace reporter Bryan writes an article for The Republican.

Teen Scene

The last couple of years have been very busy for Bryan. Now a junior in high school, his schedule is packed with activities. In addition to school and his job at *The Republican,* he also runs track. Of course, he still plays baseball. College is just on the horizon.

Wherever Bryan goes, or whatever he does, one thing is sure. He'll always be searching for a story. It excites him to have the opportunity to make a difference in the world. He writes stories that people can read, think about, and discuss with their friends. This has certainly been the effect of Bryan's newspaper column, *Teen Scene.*

One day Bryan had come up with a brainstorm: what if *The Republican* featured a column written by a teenager for teenagers? He pitched the idea to Cynthia, who was interested. *Teen Scene* was born right there on the spot. Cynthia said they would try it out and see if it caught on. The reaction has been positive. Bryan's column tackles subjects that other teenagers care about. Everybody wanted to hear his opinion about the popular website MySpace. Bryan has written columns on many topics. They include time management, school lunch programs, and youth sports.

Bryan's column is popular because he's willing to speak his mind. "I just have to tell it how I see it. That sometimes means taking an unpopular position. Being honest is important if you want your readers to respect your opinions." This is so true. That's one of the reasons that *Teen Scene* is a winner. Teenagers know they're getting the viewpoint of someone they can trust.

Success has come Bryan's way because of his character and ambition. Having a competitive spirit helps, too. Every time he has faced a challenge, he's found a way to overcome it. Like all teenagers, he has known disappointment. Still, he has a positive attitude that carries over into all parts of his life. "Red Sox fans had to wait almost a hundred years to win the World Series," he says. "I can be patient when things don't always go exactly how I want them to."

The spoils of victory: Bryan Roy, hanging out in the press box at Fenway Park, proudly displays his replica Red Sox championship ring.

With hard work, Bryan chases down his dream every day. He refuses to put limits on what he can accomplish. So, if you're ever reading a fantastic article in the newspaper or in a magazine—or maybe even reading an awesome book—check the name of the author. It might very well be Bryan Roy, athlete, Red Sox fan . . . and dedicated journalist.

Ashley Crosby, left, with her family.

Returning the Favor

Dissecting

Ashley was sure that she misunderstood what Dr. Christesen had just said. At least she hoped so. She wasn't the only one. The kids all looked around and whispered to each other. They laughed nervously, trying to figure out what to do.

Dr. Christesen just smiled patiently and waited. She wanted to give her seventh and eighth grade students a chance to get comfortable. Most people think of cats as lovable, furry creatures. Today, Dr. Christesen was going to show her students how to dissect a *dead cat*.

Dissecting means "cutting open." This is done so that doctors can look inside a dead body. By doing this, they learn many things. For example, doctors can discover new kinds of treatments for diseases.

Dissecting is important for science. Still, Dr. Christesen had known that it would make her students feel very uneasy at first. Fortunately, she had planned ahead. She had brought Lucky, her own furry cat, from home. Lucky, who was very much alive, was playful and lovable. Ashley and her friends started petting him and giving him attention. This helped them all relax. Dr. Christesen was then able to continue her lesson.

Fourteen-year-old Ashley Crosby was sitting at her desk paying close attention. She was asking questions and, as usual, taking notes. Ashley wasn't looking forward to this gross experiment. Still, nothing was going to stop her from participating. That's because this eighth grader is determined to follow her dream of helping children. She is aware that the road to becoming a doctor is long and difficult. She also knows how rewarding the result will be. This was just one small step along that road.

Dream Come True

Things ended up going pretty well. Some of the kids were still a bit uneasy, but overall it wasn't *too* bad. Dr. Christesen was pleased. The students were learning the information she was teaching them. That was the most important thing.

Ashley felt good afterward. She's never been a

big fan of blood and guts. Still, she knew this was a worthwhile project. Ashley wants to help people in the future as a doctor. So she's happy about learning as much as she can.

Ashley couldn't wait to get home that evening. She was eager to tell her mother about what she had learned . . . and how she had dissected a cat for the first time. It probably wasn't the best conversation to have during dinner. However, her mother didn't mind one bit. She knows what Ashley has overcome in her life. That's why she was happy to hear the excitement in Ashley's voice. She's proud of all the cool things her daughter does.

Hard Times

"Yeah, there have been some hard times. That just makes me appreciate what I have even more." These words of Ashley Crosby tell a lot about the kind of person she is. Remembering events from her past can be painful. She does it because she wants other kids to learn from her struggles.

As a young girl, Ashley lived in the state of Maryland with her birth mother. So did her older brother, Lawrence. Up until the time that Ashley was six years old, life was normal. She describes her early childhood as simple and fun. However, everything was set to take a tragic turn.

When Ashley was six years old, she suffered a heartbreaking loss. Her mother passed away. Ashley was with her the day she was taken to the hospital for the last time. That changed Ashley's life. It made her want to help sick people. Ashley doesn't want anyone else to go through the same thing her mother did.

Suddenly, there were no parents to care for Ashley and Lawrence. It appeared as though they would be placed in an orphanage. Ashley's grandmother, Mary Macklin, wanted to help her grandchildren. Then something happened. As Ashley explains it, "Now I know how lucky I was."

Mrs. Macklin had been a pastor in the church for twenty-six years. She was friends with a church bishop named Dr. Judy Anderson, who was a wonderful person. Not only that, but Dr. Anderson had adopted other children in the past.

Dr. Anderson heard the sad news about Ashley's mother. She didn't even hesitate. She made it clear that she would love to take care of Lawrence and Ashley. This was an incredible stroke of luck. After all, Dr. Anderson was a trusted friend of the family. Ashley's grandmother had a feeling that this situation would work out. She was right. Almost immediately, Lawrence and Ashley knew they were home.

That was many years ago. Since that time, Dr. Anderson, Lawrence, and Ashley have been a close family. They live in North Carolina, in the town of Cary. Lawrence and Ashley spend a lot of time together and help each other out. Lawrence wants to be a scientist. He is hoping to go to prestigious Yale

University.

Like his younger sister, Lawrence is an excellent student. He will definitely make it to college. There's no doubt that he's going to be successful in life. So is Ashley. As a matter of fact, she has some very big plans...

Ashley and big brother Lawrence.

Big Plans

Becoming a doctor requires years and years of school. Not only that, but many of the classes are in math and science. That's why it's lucky that Ashley enjoys these subjects and consistently earns high grades. She has her sights set on the medical school at Johns Hopkins University. That's a big plan, but Ashley is well on her way.

College, of course, is very expensive. Ashley recently received a boost from an awesome program in North Carolina. It supports kids who are on the right path. Ashley was thrilled when she was awarded a $2,000 college scholarship!

Math and science are obviously a big part of her future plans. Ashley also has a creative side, though. She loves reading. She enjoys exciting mystery novels and other types of fiction. Among her favorites is the *Lord of the Rings* series. Ashley also shows a lot of promise as a writer. She wrote a short story called "How Long is Forever." She even entered it in a writing contest at school. Her story finished in the top eight. It was also considered good enough to be entered in a national contest.

Like all teenagers in middle school, Ashley is preparing for high school. But in her case, it's a bigger and more exciting challenge than many kids face. Ashley will be attending high school and college at the same time. She's on her way to the Wake Early College of Health and Science. This college has a cool new program for incoming high school freshmen. It allows them to earn college credit while still in high school.

Ashley is looking forward to starting her new school. She wants to try different activities. For starters, she is thinking about taking a role in student government. This would be a new experience for her, but she's interested in it. She likes the idea of working with other students to bring about change. Ashley is also into sports. A good athlete, she is thinking about trying out for the track team. Her top choice is to run sprints.

The social aspect is not going to be any trouble at all. Ashley is an outgoing girl who will make a lot of friends at her new school. It's going to be an exciting time for her . . . and she can't wait!

Kicking Butt

There have been many highs and lows in Ashley Crosby's life. Yes, there were hard times. But things have turned out better than she ever could have dreamed. Everything she has been through has led to a decision: Ashley wants to make things better for children. That's more important to her than anything else.

Ashley will never forget the pain she felt after her birth mother passed away. It was also a scary time. She didn't know what was going to happen to her and Lawrence. That was followed by the joy of being adopted into a loving home. Ashley knows she was lucky. Caring people like Dr. Anderson came into her life when she needed them. Ashley has every intention of returning the favor.

She has thought about it a great deal. One way she can return the favor is by adopting children one day. That's what her mother has done. Ashley has even considered adopting a child from another country. She wants to make a difference in the life of a child by being a loving parent. She also wants to make a difference in the lives of thousands of children. She will do this through her work as a doctor.

Ashley is already doing positive things for her community. For example, she works on an anti-smoking drive called Kick Butts. She does this with her brother Lawrence. They go to meetings and plan events with other teenagers. They even planned a big event in the state capital. Kick Butts is all about trying to make kids understand the dangers of tobacco. They want kids to avoid becoming addicted to cigarettes.

Ashley and Lawrence sometimes walk into convenience stores. They remind the managers that it's illegal to sell cigarettes to minors. They ask them to sign a pledge to help kids stay away from cigarettes. Kick Butts has been a huge success so far. Ashley thinks she will stay involved for a long time to come.

With all of her extra activities, Ashley is a busy teenager. When she does have some free time, she enjoys creating origami and making jewelry. Another interest high on Ashley's list is traveling. She and her family visit Maryland whenever they have a chance. This allows Ashley and Lawrence to spend time with relatives still living there. Another of Ashley's favorite destinations is Washington, D.C. She loves going to the science and art museums. There are plenty of awesome exhibits to look at. The museums collect and display the coolest stuff on the planet.

It's clear that Ashley and Lawrence enjoy traveling. They also like hanging out with family and friends. A recent event took place that was very special to Ashley. One of her stepsisters adopted a little boy named Ishawn. Ashley, who is terrific with children, loves to play with her little nephew.

There's another person Ashley and Lawrence love spending time with—their grandmother, Mary Macklin. Now elderly and blind, Mrs. Macklin lives in a nursing home. Ashley keeps her company. This is the caring side of Ashley that is headed for a career helping people. Mrs. Macklin took care of her a long time ago. Now Ashley is happy that she is returning the favor.

Proud moment: Future doctor Ashley Crosby graduates from middle school.

Returning the favor is what Ashley is all about. That will certainly be the case when she is an adult. The lucky people will be children who come under her care. They will have a wonderful doctor. Ashley is devoted to making the world a better place.

Through good times and bad, Ashley Crosby has never lost sight of her dreams. She gets excellent grades so she can go to a fine college. She believes in "kicking butt" so that kids won't smoke. And, of course, she takes care of her elderly grandmother. Ashley has set upon a course that will touch everyone she comes into contact with. Fifteen or twenty years into the future, you may just need a good doctor. If so, just pick up the phone and book an appointment with Dr. Ashley Crosby!

2 fast 4 U

Teen Court

Sixteen-year-old K.L. Cleeton arrived at the courthouse. He was given a piece of paper called a docket. It described the cases that would be heard in court that evening. The first case involved a shoplifting incident. The second case was about alcohol.

It was the third case, however, that caught K.L.'s eye. It seemed strange. A fifteen-year-old boy named Timothy Jenkins was on trial. He was being accused of attacking another person and causing injury. According to the police report, Timothy had hurt his stepmother. K.L. wondered what the story was behind this incident.

Sixteen-year-old K.L. Cleeton in front of the Effingham County Courthouse.

K.L. was at a real courthouse. He was about to act as a lawyer in real court cases. That's because he participates in Teen Court. This is a program offered in his hometown of Effingham, Illinois. Teen Court is designed for teenagers who break the law. Instead of Juvenile Court, they appear in Teen Court. There, the lawyers and jury are teenagers! For K.L., it's a great opportunity to learn about the law. This is the career he plans to pursue in the future.

K.L. Cleeton is following his dream of becoming a lawyer. Nothing will stop him, not even the physical challenges he faces every day. He simply won't let them slow him down. That's the mark of a teenager who isn't afraid of taking risks. Sure, some people might look at him differently at first because he's in a wheelchair. That used to be difficult for K.L. to deal with. Not anymore. He has learned to rise above the curious stares. Once people get to know him, they quickly forget about his wheelchair.

The stakes are high in Teen Court. There's nothing make-believe about the process. A kid who is on trial—like Timothy Jenkins—needs a skilled attorney. Luckily, Timothy had one . . . K.L. Cleeton.

The Trial of Timothy Jenkins

In Teen Court, several trials take place over the course of one night. Things move quickly. The lawyers have to be focused because they work under a ton of pressure. K.L. would have to ask questions and try to find out important details.

The first two cases were simple because none of the facts were in dispute. In the shoplifting case, a security camera showed that Johnny Williams had stolen something. He tried to leave a store with an expensive shirt tucked inside his jacket. The teenagers on the jury found Johnny guilty. They sentenced him to fifteen hours of community service.

The second case was also simple. A police officer had spotted sixteen-year-old Bill Carter and two friends late at night. They were drinking alcohol by the tennis courts at the park. The jury showed little mercy. Bill received twenty hours of community service.

Next, the trial of Timothy Jenkins began. It seemed that this would be an easy case. There was a lot of evidence against him. He had actually confessed to the police. It looked like it was going to be a pretty dull night in Teen Court.

The first lawyer to speak was fifteen-year-old Clarissa Hart. She began by telling the jury about the police report. It painted an ugly picture for Timothy. The police had responded to a call from a neighbor. They had arrived at the Jenkins's home to find Mrs. Jenkins with some bad bruises.

According to the report, Timothy had been on the computer in the living room. He was chatting online with friends. His stepmother told him that he had to sign off. Timothy became very angry. An argument took place, and apparently that's when the attack happened.

Clarissa asked Timothy questions that made him look guilty. "Did you and your stepmother get into a big argument?" When Timothy responded yes, the people in the audience whispered to each other. This wasn't looking good for him.

K.L. carefully studied Timothy's face. The teenager was talking softly and responding only "yes" and "no" to questions. K.L. had a gut feeling that there was more to the story. Quickly looking at the police report, K.L. noticed several interesting facts. He impatiently waited for his turn to speak.

Finally, Clarissa turned to the judge. "No further questions, your Honor," she announced. The judge turned to K.L. and said, "Your turn, Mr. Cleeton." Everybody in the courtroom looked at K.L. Timothy had already admitted guilt—what could his lawyer possibly do?

Positive Outcome

K.L. started out by asking, "Timothy, do you have a bad temper?"

Looking down, Timothy softly responded, "No."

"I know you don't, because I've been studying your file." K.L. paused for a moment. Then he continued, "You've never been in trouble with the police. You're also a straight A student. You've never even gotten detention at school." Nobody had any idea why K.L. was saying these things. This case was starting to get interesting.

K.L. asked, "Timothy, I noticed something else in your file. Is it true that your stepmother has been arrested several times before? Always for alcohol and drugs?"

Timothy's face turned bright red. He hadn't expected this subject to come up. Before he could respond, K.L. looked at the members of the jury. "Does this really make sense?" he asked. "Timothy is a good person. He's never been in trouble before. Why would he suddenly attack a family member? Just because he had to turn off the computer? I don't think so."

K.L. moved forward until he was only a few feet away from the jury. "Something doesn't add up," he said quietly. "Why would Timothy lie and get punished? *Why*? What if he's taking the heat for someone else? Someone who was drunk. Maybe his stepmother fell down the stairs. Maybe she tripped and bumped her head. We don't know. But, ladies and gentlemen, keep one thing in mind—this is someone who could be sent to jail if she were to get arrested again."

Turning sharply to look at Timothy, K.L. said loudly, "Timothy, what *really* happened?"

Tears started forming in Timothy's eyes. He tried to control it, but all of a sudden he broke down. It seemed like he was relieved to finally tell the truth. "It's not her fault," he sobbed, looking at the jury for the first time. "She's tried to quit drinking. I didn't want anything bad to happen to her. We're a family."

For a moment, there was confusion in the court-room. Everybody was whispering to each other. The judge had to pound his gavel to restore order. This was an amazing turn of events.

K.L. felt sorry for Timothy. He knew that Timothy had learned an important lesson about lying. Timothy's stepmother wasn't a criminal, but she obviously needed help. Lying about the situation wasn't doing her any good.

Happily, there was a positive outcome. Timothy's stepmother wasn't sent to jail; instead, she agreed to get help for her drinking problem. Because of K.L. Cleeton, she was on the road to getting better.

The judge told the jury that he was throwing the case out of court. Timothy Jenkins was free to leave, with no punishment at all. The truth—and the skill of his lawyer—had set him free.

Fascination with Politics

K.L. Cleeton has always been interested in law and politics. One of the highlights of his life took place in 2004. He had the opportunity to go to a presidential debate. K.L. and his father drove from Illinois to St. Louis. They were there to watch President George W. Bush square off against Senator John Kerry.

It was a wild scene outside the auditorium. People, shouting and carrying signs, lined the streets.

This is known as a protest, or a demonstration. Police, in full riot gear, stood nearby. They made sure things didn't get out of hand.

The debate itself was unforgettable. K.L. had a fantastic time at this historic event. "It made me think," he says. "My dream would be to represent the state of Illinois as a senator. Or maybe even my country as the president."

K.L., posing with his father, attending a historic event—a presidential debate.

K.L.'s fascination with politics got even stronger because of a cool thing that happened. He met a famous politician from his own state of Illinois. One day he had to leave school early because he had an appointment with the dentist. It just so happened that the governor was in town to make a speech. His name was Rod Blagojevich [pronounced bluh-goy-uh-vich]. K.L. asked his dad if they could go and watch.

Friends in high places: K.L. meets Governor Blagojevich.

After delivering his speech, the governor noticed K.L. in the front row. He came up to him and shook his hand. K.L. smiled. He mentioned that he wouldn't mind having the governor's job one day. Mr. Blagojevich smiled back at him. He said, "Well, in that case, why don't you come and visit me one day? You can come to the governor's mansion in Spring-field."

K.L. was thrilled. A few weeks later he received a handwritten invitation from the governor. He's eagerly looking forward to this exciting trip. He can't wait to see the governor again.

2 fast 4 U

"Don't ever make excuses . . . I've met a lot of people that are physically challenged. Sometimes they say, 'I can't do it,' and I'm like, 'dude, *yes* you can.' I feel like I can do anything if I try hard enough." These words tell a lot about the kind of person K.L. Cleeton is. Sure, he may have some physical limitations. But the sky's the limit as far as what he can accomplish in life.

Kenneth Lloyd Cleeton would come to be known as K.L. He was only six months old when doctors made a discovery. K.L. had a disease known as spinal muscular atrophy. It was a difficult period for Mr. and Mrs. Cleeton. They were told that their son likely wouldn't live. But K.L. has always had a fighting spirit. He bucked the odds and survived. He's gone on to become a popular and awesome teenager.

K.L. understands that there are some things he won't be able to do. He just focuses on all the incredible things he *has* done—and will continue to do. "I don't have any regrets," he explains. "None at all. If you have regrets, that means you missed out on something you wanted to do. And then your life wasn't as full as it could have been. I'm not the kind of kid that's going to just sit here and stare at a wall. I've got too much going on!" He sure does. K.L. has Teen

Court and his interest in politics. In addition to all that, he has fun hobbies that any kid can relate to.

One thing K.L. gets into is speed, as in, "Things that go fast!" A big NASCAR fan, he gets a kick out of watching the Speed channel. K.L. has hung out with famous NASCAR champion Tony Stewart! "It was cool," K.L. says. "We talked about video games, racing, and a bunch of other stuff. Tony is awesome."

As much as K.L. likes NASCAR, his very favorite type of racing is flat track. He describes it as "NASCAR on motorcycles." Flat track is an exciting sport. It features motorcycle racing on a track with a dirt surface.

K.L. has also become friends with many of the flat track riders. He recently traveled to Ohio to watch a race. His good friend, seven-time grand national champion Chris Carr, was racing.

K.L. and his buddy, Chris Carr.

Another person K.L. loves to hang out with is his younger brother Kyler. They like playing video games and doing things online together. Often times Kyler will just pick K.L. up and carry him to the living room. That way, they can watch a movie together.

K.L. is racing through his life at a fast pace. It's like Tony Stewart at a championship NASCAR event! Just check out the license plate on the back of K.L.'s wheelchair. It was a birthday present from his mom. Mrs. Cleeton saw it at a NASCAR race in North Carolina. She thought of K.L. right away. It simply says, "2 fast 4 U." What a perfect way to describe K.L.

Yes, nature has forced K.L. Cleeton to deal with some huge challenges. But it has also given him a strong spirit. That's what makes him an inspiration to everyone he meets. Whether K.L. ends up becoming a lawyer, or even a president, one thing is sure: K.L. Cleeton will definitely make this world a better place. He's got a creative and unique view of the world. Maybe that's why he'll probably always be just a little bit "2 fast 4 U!"